Wolves

Written by Sandra Iversen

Wolves are animals
that look like big dogs.
Most wolves have silver-brown fur.
Other wolves have black or white fur.
They have big teeth and yellow eyes.

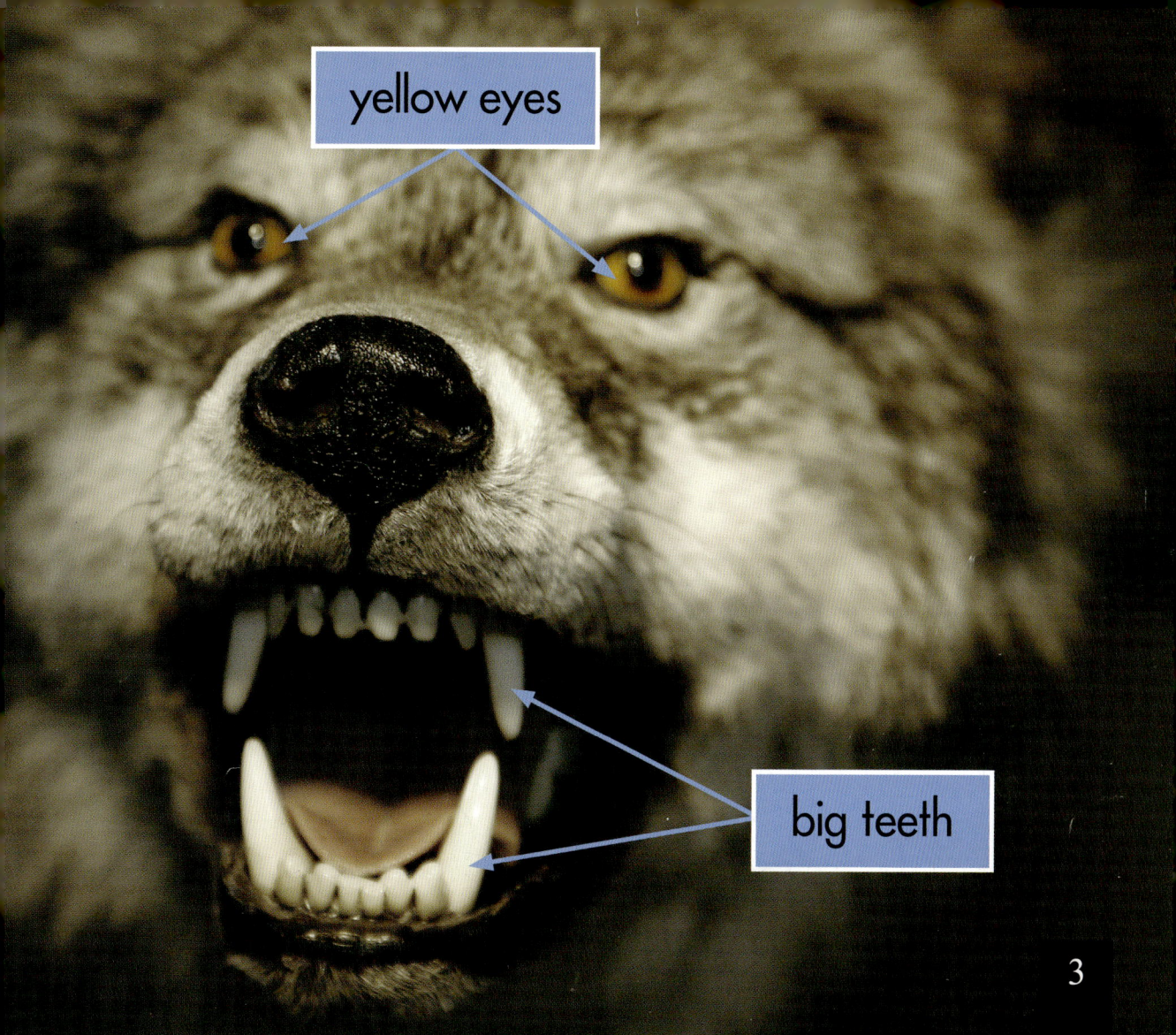

Wolves live in packs.
Some packs have four wolves in them.
Other packs are bigger.
Wolves hunt for food in packs.
They eat sheep and goats.
They also eat pigs and deer.
They prowl around looking for prey.
They pounce on their prey and bite it.
Their big teeth can crush bones.

Wolves howl to let other wolves
in the pack know where they are.
They howl to keep other packs
of wolves away.
They howl in the breeding season.

wolves howling

You can hear a wolf howl
just before it gets dark.
You can hear them howl at night, too.
You can hear the howls
a long way away.

Wolf pups are born in a den.
They cannot see or hear.
They stay in the den for about two months.
Pups learn to bark when they want food.
They learn to growl and howl.
They growl when they are angry.
They howl when they come out of the den.

Index

den. 10

hunt 4

pack(s) 4, 6

prey 4

pups. 10

wolves 2, 4, 6